I Love You
Kiss Me Goodnight

memoire in the form of a big poem

Kathryn Kimiecik Foley

ACKNOWLEDGMENTS

Thank you, Nick Marco, for a decade of mentorship.

CHAPTER ONE

JUNE

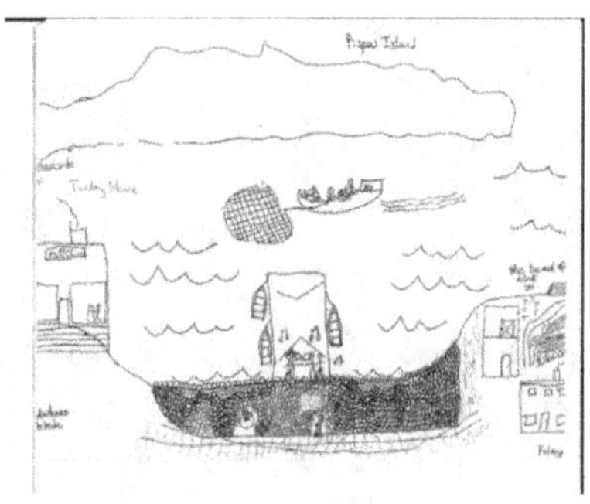

June

1.

The young men whistle as I go by
they see a woman who is mysterious only because she is there,
where she has never been before

Their curiosity is high
but their actions reveal only their fear of a new woman

She walks past the wharf
her heart pounds because she too is afraid
afraid of being stared at
afraid of not being able to understand them and
afraid she never will

She tells herself she will never walk past them again
but it's a lie

They look at her and she can't speak
She has become more quiet with these men than
she ever thought possible

What is she afraid of
is it their sexuality
or her own

2.

He sings and smiles
teaches and gives
He wants her to learn and isn't angry when she's quiet
He knows it takes time but's willing to persist, and does
He encourages her by simply being

She has never felt so much honest love pour out of her

Her love for him is borne of the knowledge that he is content with
her and doesn't strain her capabilities

She's young and scared and has much to learn
She's always saturated with the newness of her environment

CHAPTER TWO

JULY

July 11

3.

I sit here
angry that I'm not free
angry that I'm not with him
The radio blares noise that is not Simani
The DJ is a jerk who's not capable

4.

We come back amazed that nothing has changed
yet I will never be the same
We eat at McDonald's wonder
where the reality has crept in
Are the people here any less real?
No they are real in an artificial world
A world that doesn't include sunsets that are like
the first time you realized
you were loved by someone special

5.

He smiles, looks for approval
We make plans for the rest of the summer
hope that some of them work out
I'm afraid that sometimes his imagination wanders to
an incredible fantasy level

He wants to sing, to write
He says for the first time
	What a team
and I'm elated

6.

We laugh and smile
Shake our heads at our new world
wonder what happened to suburbs and farms
Do they still exist?
Are they as unreal as my life here?
Is The Cove reality or is it

I prefer that life
rocks and cliffs and boxes
birds and breasts and Bruce

We listen to Bruce first thing
Sometimes I cringe at his accuracy

My lover loves the depression; I don't understand
I tell him I worry about him
he could destroy himself
I tell him I worry about him
he laughs
but I've said it
and now he understands it's true

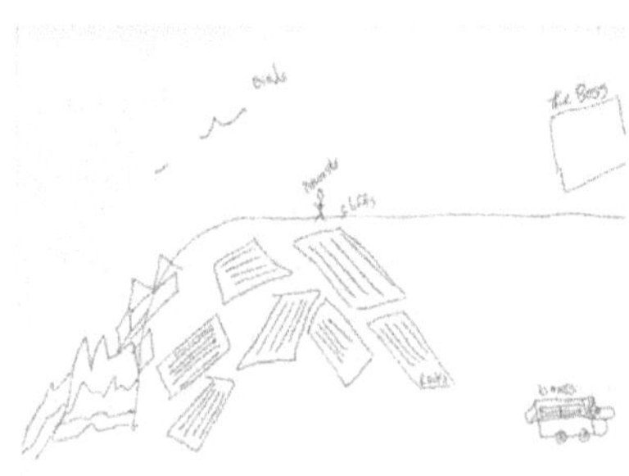

7.

He is supposed to pick me up,
he's late
he calls

       Is it too late to go? He asks
       No, I tell him
I need to see him
I haven't seen him all day
He's wearing his muscle shirt and looks great
I feel like a schoolgirl when
I know he's trying to be cool
He's the coolest nerd I've ever seen

He picks me up
       I could have been doing my laundry
       Fuck the laundry
we both laugh

He loves being in crazy situations
He glows when the scene is absurd
and I love him when he glows

I'm always amazed I'm his choice for craziness
We curse and swear at the crazy people in The Cove
I say
       We are crazier

We love the same things,
and without saying it
know that we thrive on each other
I'm embarrassed when others we know see us together

I know they're speculating
even though nothing has been said yet

I'm asked
       Are you coming home tonight?

I feign shock
but am delighted in a stupid way
I feel flattered that people think
I could have a relationship with him
is this stuff all bullshit
I like to think it's not

He's good for my heart and my head
I'm not lonely anymore
and yet,
I know I will be when I go

July 17

8.

I'm alright on the bus
I tell myself if I was going to cry
I should have in The Cove
I stopped myself then

The ride is long and as long as we move
I'm unaware of my destination
I'm semi-conscious

We still move, but now
I see only lights and no stars

The lights become more explicit
They laugh at me
know I hate them

I begin to cry
all the lights scare me
I think of all the people who are here and cringe
There isn't enough room,
I shout in my head
My head explodes in pain and I sob
I see the Village and Sobeys and Woolco
and am unable to comprehend

    That's your world
he's told me
But is it?
Why then do I cringe at the sight?
Why are my tears uncontrolled as
the neon flashes and glares at me?

My traveling companion tries to comfort me
and she does a bit

We laugh at ourselves
wonder what the hell has been going on

I open my door and there is the electric bill
I ignore it because it too is real
and I want only to feel the unreal
reality of the past few days

I pick up the phone and I call him
I need to tell him I'm alright
that I'll make it

He says
        Oh my God
And I feel wonderful knowing he's glad to hear me
        How was the bus ride
        Alright, but bad; well not bad. I didn't cry until I saw the friggin' mall.
He laughs,
and I'm there with him

9.

We are at Frank's
I hand him a beer
      It's warm, I say
      Like me, says he

10.

I interrupt him
        I have this bizarre craving
        for kielbasa and pierogis

11.

My local hero

12.

I used to think I was from New York

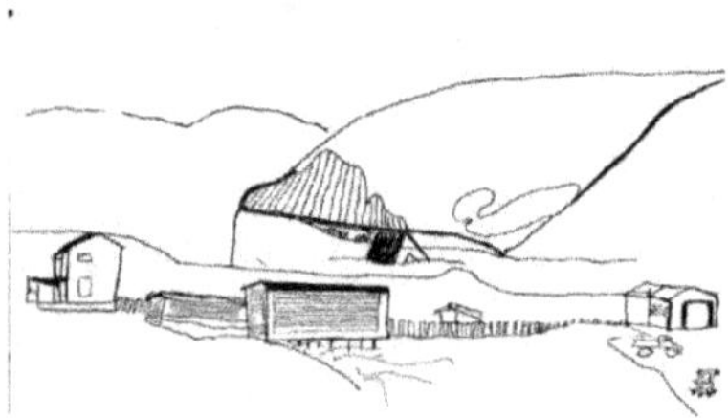

13.

I barely make it to the rocks
I'm dazed and I cry
They are tears of pain and joy
        It's too extreme! explodes in my head

The sun is rising and here am I
unable to comprehend my own emotions
All I can do is feel

He comes to me
and my arms reach out
to draw him into my agony

I cling to him
not able to get close enough
not able to hide my fear of beauty
I use him as a shield from the scene
that surrounds me
and scares me

    It hurts, I tell him
    What hurts? He asks
my tears flow harder

My eyes are blinded
and I can only feel
only touch
and be touched

        At least you don't smell like Brut 33, I say
He laughs
We lay back
I'm quiet in his arms
knowingly content for the first time in my life

Behind us is a low strip of orange

in front of us is the moon,
not yet set
as crisp and clear as I now feel

The moment is like us
different things happen at once

he turns from
father to lover

He kisses me and I'm no longer afraid
He's soft and loving
concerned for me

I feel his tongue for the first time
my body and brain respond
He touches my breast
and I no longer belong to this world

crunch crunch on the rocks
      Is that Karen, says he
      Yea
      I don't believe this; it's too bizarre
We're not embarrassed and laugh softly together
feel no guilt
just love
      Ah, yes, well, I see, she says,
      and she leaves

He kisses me again
and I am home

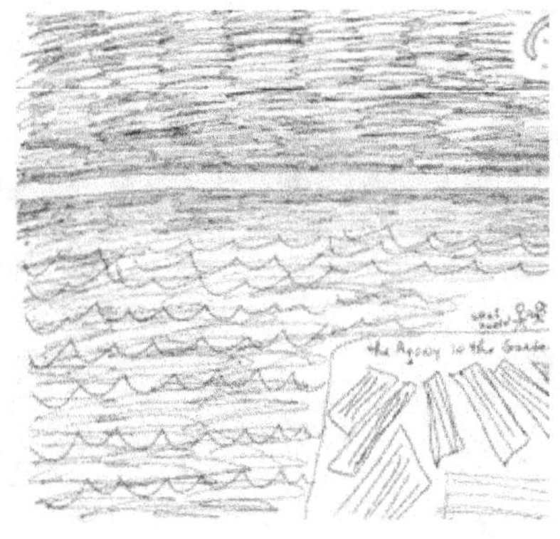
the Agony in the Garden

14.

>I remember in the fall
>how appalled I was when you said
>you didn't think of back home as home anymore.

>Are you appalled now? he asks

I shake my head,
understand,
or at least start to

July 18

15.

I sit here at the laundromat
like an automaton
I fill machines insert quarters
fill machines insert quarters
fill machines insert quarters

I think of Nellie doing the wash
and stop complaining
          Fuck the laundry, he once said, he's right

I search all day for technological objects,
amazed at the stupidity which they think is reality
Why don't I leave
I have responsibilities
Fuck the responsibilities

16.

I've always felt that you were part of the family

17.

Like the washing machines
my eyes fill
I want to call him to find out what he's doing this very minute
Is he with the kids up the lane?
Is he with me?

> Are you kidding? I'm not going to see those guys until
> you get back, says he
> You knows he ain't that kind, says Frank
> Tell Frank I know that for sure now.
> I'm not going to repeat that

18.

You're some precious, says I

19.

I drink pepsi
buy my lunch

I buy a bottle of Chianti and fry some cod tongues
Wish it was Monday night

Our passion was intense
out of our control
Never before have I had such a lover
He's knowledgeable
I don't want to know how he has arrived at such wisdom
I'm only glad he does what he does

His mouth is on my lips
his tongue searches for my wetness
and creates even more
My mind reels
I'm barely conscious
My body contorts wildly with his pressure
My arms reach out for infinity, for sanity
I feel I can't take anymore but I do
He frees himself from all constraints
I feel him gasp and want him inside me

No man has ever reacted like that with me before
For the first time in my life
I feel like the woman he says I am
> For the past three days I ask, who is this
> person? Is she my daughter, my sister, my
> lover?

I can't believe he's saying these things
I too have felt those same emotions for him
but have been unable to articulate it

> Who is this person?, he says

Is she my daughter, sister, lover,
and I realized she was a woman.

I feel his mouth on mine
and I'm no longer able to write.

20.

I stand outside the laundromat
the sun has begun to set
I cry because I'm not there
I know he's on the rocks this very instant
watching, feeling

I look at the sky
know the exact position of our place on the rocks,
know where the moon will eventually rise and set
know where Venus will be in the morning.

He is all these things,
skies and stars
and sun.

21.

I sit here and the noise is unbearable.
My brain screams for silence,
but there's no answer

There are oil fumes but I desire only to
smell the fish guts in The Cove
only to breathe in the scent of my lover,
his skin damp with moisture.

22.

I sit here, outside a building which has no rightful
place on this earth.

I've learned the most important things on the rocks,
without book or pencil.

23.

I've changed
I can feel it
My aloneness is no longer lonely, because I'm with you.

I once told him he would destroy himself.
This time I told him
I never thought I would destroy my self.

Now I know it was not destruction,
rather it was a growth I was afraid of.
I've been built up,
not shattered.

July 20

24.

I wait to leave,
my heart pounds with expectancy.
The sun shines its radiance on me
or do I shine on it?

Are you ready to see me
I wonder how you will act
father brother lover

firebirds and feathers
lobster and liquor

I go to the store to buy fancy cheese for tomorrow's supper

It's times like these when I feel as sister, friend.
How then do I become lover
I wonder how incestuous our
relationship is

He ruffles my hair and I feel like his daughter
he caresses my hair,
and I become his lover

Hours are wasted waiting to leave
I could be on the rocks listening and looking,
no longer afraid of the beauty before me.

I'm tired
I don't sleep well here
I only want to lay in the sunshine of The Cove
where the sounds are not noise
sheep and chickens
boats and water
voices and song

25.

I wake in the morning to his voice.
He sings from the kitchen
knows I listen.
What great way to wake up
My body fills with the warmth his presence creates.
Again, I wonder,
how did I end up here,
who is this man who cares for me

I lay in bed while the rain on the roof
romances me.

I curl under my sheet,
think, what a great day to stay in bed.

He comes upstairs to see if I'm awake.
he sits by me and plays with my hair
What a great day to stay in bed.

26.

I barely make it to the rocks but
this time I'm no longer afraid
I'm ecstatic to see and
Touch those who I love

the rocks speak to me
they know I listen
He waits for me at the house,
understands my emotions better
than I do
Later, he tells me,
      I said to Frank, the first thing she's going to do
      is go to the rocks.
he's right

27.

    Fortunately or unfortunately, I don't come here
    just to see you.

    Well, that's good.

    You're perceptive. I don't want to fuck that up; I don't want to destroy
    your mind.

We talk in the stable,
children hang around.
We're oblivious to them
concerned only with each other.

He speaks to me
about me

July 28.

28.

We decide not to make love anymore
I'm going crazy
I can't stand it here anymore

29.

May your home always be filled with the love of friends,
Like you've filled mine.

30.

      I just want to be near you.

We sleep together,
know our caresses are from love,
understand each other's restraint.

Chapter Three

August

August 15, 1:15 a.m.

31.

      I'm sorry I'm so bitter. I can tell you're losing
      your patience with me. I feel bad enough
      without causing you superficial pain. You'll have to excuse me
      but I don't know how many more times
      I'll be able to touch your face.

      Not many, said he sarcastically.

Right now I hate you and I hate myself.
I'm near tears because once again
I'm on the wrong side of life.
I've never been able to call the shots,
least of all when I want to most.

Why do I put myself through this torture.
I should leave tomorrow but I can't because
being near you is all I care about.
The pain is still greater when I'm unable to look at you at all.

I know it's wrong to expect you to make love to me.
I hate you for putting me through this.
Why was I unwise enough to stop before anything started.

Lately I've begun to feel as if I bore you.
Have I changed so much that I've become uninteresting?

You once said I was different, told me you loved me
that you were concerned about me.
Now when I need you the most,
you run scared,
throw me aside
You never touch me at all
You've gone from one extreme to the other
but then you always were into extremes, weren't you?

I cry a lot lately but you never seem to notice.

Are you scared of me,
afraid of what I represent
afraid to deal with your own lust and carnality
afraid to remember what we had with each other

afraid of the love we felt for each other,
whether it involved sex or not.

I can deal with no sex,
I don't want sex.
I want you to talk to me
tell me that we can be, and are friends.
You once said you'd hate to fuck up my life
well you are but not because of no sex.
It's because you've pushed me
out of your mind

Whatever happened to me
whatever happened to the concern you said
you've always felt for me
whatever happened to the man who told me he felt as
though I was part of the family
where is that man
why do you hid from me

I need you to talk to me
don't block me out

32.

am I annoying you?
I don't know.
then I am.

33.

You act as if nothing ever happened between us at all
How can you ignore all that
I'm not asking you to return to that status, I just don't want
you to forget there was an awful lot of love between us

You once said you loved a lot of people
I know that but once I was included in that group

How did you go from lover to stranger

34.

I love you, I can't make love to you. It's absurd, I say

35.

No longer will I let you make love to me here
I look only to the future now
That's all I want
a future,
whether or not it's sexual

I was afraid somehow I'd never see you elsewhere
afraid that you wouldn't want to see me, ever
your love has calmed me
I know wherever you are
you will love me

I know there are things that will never let you forget me
things too that will make me think of you, and I will smile
memories are wonderful things
many of them will hurt,
and I'll still suffer for a time yet

Only when I forget your love
do I fall deeper into fear, and my tears flow
In times like that I will force myself to remember
the peacefulness
you've given me

Your love, because it's so powerful, frightens me,
sometimes painful
but it's also the depth of it
which gives me the strength
to defeat my fear,
to simply feel the passion and depth of my own emotions.

36.

I often wonder whether this is poetry
I don't know anything about poetry
You've created this
And thanks for that

37.

My mind reels because I have a history of unrequited love
Your words last night chased that fear away
Three times in one minute you told me you loved me
I couldn't answer
my happiness spoke for me
Never before has anyone left me so totally speechless
When you said those words to me first
I realized that you do indeed love me
Sometimes a girl gets scared
She will say
      I love you
And then wonder if the response is just habitual
That's why,
when you say
I love you
to me,
without any prompts
I understand it's true.

38.

You ask
      what are your plans
I say
      I'm not coming back
he says
      What do you want me to tell my wife

You play quietly with my new kitten
the house is filled with love and children's laughter
I can feel the love when I walk through the gate.
It pulls me in and I'm unable to resist,
very like you.

You sleep on the couch
Warren howls on the radio
In the kitchen are tomatoes and lettuce from
your back garden

Today was the first time you went somewhere
without me in the truck
I preferred that today because
I knew you'd be happy to see me when you got back

The kids rush in
but I hush them
hope to please you
I'm always conscious of wanting you to be happy.

Lately I can see you've begun to doubt
your desire for complete honesty
and that's very wrong
What is it that compels us to be honest
yet know we are going to cause
pain
anger
fear

39.

Our mouths barely touch
We breathe softly on each other,
prolong our desire
My eyes shut while my heart opens
(among other things)
I lay against you and feel your
penis hard and throbbing
      Oh my God, you state, you're not wearing a bra
and you breathe deeply

August 23

40.

We stand by the bus
know real fear and love at the same moment
My eyes are filled with tears,
like the sea water at The Cove, it burns them
People have begun to watch our goodbye.
for an instant
I tell myself
I'm being melodramatic
but it isn't so

Your hand is on my shoulder
  Don't cry, you suggest
  Don't worry, I'll wait till I get on the bus

One last hug,
and I pull away, unable to speak
I see only your face expressing
the love between us
My back is turned to you
but I feel your voice behind me
  I love you, you say
I nearly collapse from hearing your voice
I step up, turn to speak to you with my eyes,
say more than I ever could with my voice

I take one last step,
being pushed further and further away from you
I can't remove my eyes from your soul
You smile at me with your whole body
We make crazy gestures that only we understand

I'm annoyed that I have to sit with someone, on the aisle no less
My body shakes from my deep sense of loss
the tears flow on

I see your face desperately
looking for me but trying to stay cool
You are, after all, wearing a new earring
You circle the bus
my head screams for you to find me
No longer can I take it and I run to the front of my prison, say
              I'm on the other side, up towards the front but I'm on the aisle.
This time you walk around
our eyes catch through the brown glass between us
My tears flow,
now from the
happiness which you've so freely given me

We laugh at ourselves through our barrier,
unable to stop looking at each other,
into each other's eyes.
My tears have stopped and I feel sure now
that we will both survive whatever
it is we have to
We both know that regardless of the future
we will always love each other for what was
and not for what could have been

41.

We dance slowly in the kitchen
Our bodies are joined at the hips
You place your hands on my waist
I slowly rub your long hips with my fingers
Your mouth is on my hair and when you breathe on me
my vagina contracts deep within me

I close my eyes,
only to see you stand naked before me
I rub your shoulders as my
mouth moves across your chest
My tongue licks you in places
I have no control over
Your hands touch my hardened nipples,
while your tongue
has found mine
I feel the length of your body and
the more dominating length of your penis
My vagina feels heavy and full
my inner thighs are soaked with my wetness
Simultaneously your hand finds
my clitoris
tries to collect the moisture you created,
while my fingers wrap themselves around
your penis and your balls
I'm always amazed at the coolness of your testicles
especially when compared with the heat your penis gives off
Each time your fingers slide inside me and you press my clitoris,
I grip your penis harder from the convulsion my body experiences
Both sets of lips open and I want you thrusting inside me

I open my eyes and we're both fully clothed.
Your hands are still on my waist
your legs are covered in silk
        How was that, you inquire
I shake my head to clear my brain

Are you ready to go? He adds
The light is turned off
the door is shut

August 26 was the Sunday we left

August 27, Monday morning

42.

I've surrounded myself with their faces
their expressions caught with a machine that reveals
their happiness and love

I look at each face and study it
I hear their voices all the time
but rather than disturb me those sounds comfort me
because I know those voices are still alive even
when I'm not there

Their faces are frozen in laughter
our faces,
though we are often worlds apart
match theirs in love and peace
it's when you and I smile with our hearts
that we become their equals

43.

I sit in my room
amazed that I can attain some level of calm
I've been physically sick all day
I want to know
yet don't want to know

I've relived yesterday a thousand times
the painful walk to Frank's house
the talk with young Queen,
the talk with you
> It's been the best summer of my life, it's The Cove, says he
> I want you to know that I'm grateful I was a small part of the
> best summer of your life, says I
> You were a major part, he assures me

I danced with tears in my eyes because
I was so aware of your happiness
I've said before that I love you when you glow
and glow you did Saturday night

44.

We're finally on our way

My eyes are bleary
bloodshot
swollen
you turn our music on
I pray we don't see anybody else on the road

You drive past the shop for one last look
we both know you will be back soon but
it will never be the same for either of us
I'm afraid to look out across the harbour,
to your home
to my home
I force myself to take one last glance
and it makes me hurt

No one is seen as we drive away except
one teenager whose
emotions will never let him say I love you, to me
He's alone on his bike
waits only for us
he smiles and waves as we go by
and follows for a bit
there is something so sad,
and yet so utterly beautiful about his gesture
that it is this final act that breaks me completely
I'm numbed by his kindness,
which was,
for him,
a tribute to us and summer's end
He didn't need to say I love you
and I understand now that I didn't need to hear it
only to feel it

45.

I wear Bruce to sleep
I think of you constantly, wait for the sharpness to fade
I am reminded of our last night together when you said
      I don't want to screw you, I just want to be near you

We still excite each other
but I feel a peacefulness now because neither one of us
wants to make love
there's too much to lose

I told you once very long ago in the stable
that we had a relationship before without sex,
and that we can do it again
Now I know we've succeeded.
Even if I never see you again,
or feel you breathe in my bed
I know we've succeeded
and I love you as I have never loved another human being before
and I will love you forever in a way that
I will never love another man

46.

The zucchini was wonderful
garlic
onions
tomatoes
cauliflower
cheese sauce
Valpolicella
and you

August 29, Wednesday night

47.

I open my window as high as it will go
hope the air will cool my mind and my body
It does neither

The traffic is unbearable
I long to hear just one truck,
a truck that raises gravel and dust in the lane
I want to be able to identify the driver,
not feel overwhelmed by the volume of cars

All individuality is lost here
we must constantly fight to
maintain our own level of
creativity and private thought

There's no one here I can talk to
I need to express my exhilaration of my new self
I need to tell somebody
but nobody can hear

I've had a thousand conversations with you,
only you don't know it
they remain in my head.
I have so many questions to ask you
but because you're not here,
I forget them

48.

It's funny how parts of this summer already feel like years ago
like the first time you kissed me on the rocks
it was so pure
it was simple basic emotion, and nothing else
I remember how childlike your enthusiasm was the night
we took the tape recorder,
our favorite music,
a blanket
and a bottle of wine to the rocks
and how you ever so lightly touched my ankle all the while
Tom and Ken
were up there throwing rocks over the cliffs
or how happy and surprised you were
when I reacted as I did to your lovemaking
or how you used to wake me up in the morning by singing
I always woke up and immediately smiled
Sometimes you came upstairs and sat on my bed
And played softly with my hair

49.

I tell you all day
I love you
and sometimes make believe
that wherever you are
you hear me,
and answer

I like to think that my words echo in your mind from times past
even if it is only once in a while
I hope you can hear me
I love you

50.

I've grown more used to your absence
I still look for you but don't really expect to see you
I spend my days alone,
even when I'm with people.
I work hard,
so hard that the days go quickly
It's the nights that are still difficult
I wake often and for
long periods of time
I've forgotten your scent but would know it instantly.
When it's light
I awake,
half hear you and
your grandfather groan

I lay in my bed
Hear your movements in the room below
and then I open my eyes
How sad I am

How wonderful it is to be awakened
by someone you love,
to feel love simply because it's there, in the house,
is something I miss
There is no love in this room
It's large and empty and hollow
You would make it cozy and full and vibrant
It's become a daily struggle for me to leave my bed
How many times have I refused for an hour or more

I dreamed once that you had died
You and my kitten were submerged under a wave
that refused to recede
I stood on a cliff, among strangers

I turned my back for a moment,
when I looked again
all was gone,
under water.
I could feel you gasp for air
I screamed at the wave to go back
but it wouldn't listen
no one ever does,
except you
I left with the strangers
They told me there was nothing I could do

You came back from the dead later on,
in the same dream
No one was surprised,
least of all you

I remember seeing your earring
You shrugged your shoulders, like you do
You looked at me but nothing was communicated
I awoke
and was afraid

51.

I sit in the bar among friends who are strangers
I laugh, but not at their jokes
I laugh at myself for hating them
Our talk is always latent with arrogant sexuality
A male mentions how attractive he finds his own arms
They are strong and veined, like yours
How can I help but think of you
how your arms feel when they're wrapped around my body
How can I not think of your grandfather,
who you loved and still do.

52.

I am lonely and need a hug very badly
I wonder how much (if at all)
you think about me
I don't want to screw you
I just want to be near you

53.

I awake with a heaviness on my body
I've dreamed of you
I stay in bed because that is where I feel you the most
When I'm there
I'm safe
because I hide from the reality
which is our world
My mind skips over scenes,
both bad and good
I think of how good some of the bad ones were
I think of the powerfulness of emotion
and I'm glad I've shared that with you

My problem now
is that I'm constantly happy and sad at the same time
I don't understand it but I feel it
My mind shifts from memories of our love and care
to the hatefulness I feel for not being able to express it

I want others to know what I've gone through
want them to be able to see the change in me
but they won't because I can't let them
I wonder if perhaps they'll see it in other ways
ways that I'm not aware of

54.

        Let's go dancing, a friend says.
It's 6 o'clock in the evening.
        I don't really feel like it, I said.

I go anyway because I know I must
The bar is empty but we don't wait for it to fill up
we dance anyway,
an entire floor to ourselves
I keep thinking of you
You'd love the space

I request Bruce
the tears begin to flow
I dance with no one but for you
I dance for the summer
and dance for myself

I am reminded of our dance at East Cove
and dance with you
I feel your presence
I feel the scene in the truck
on the last trip

A spiritual experience, you called it
I can feel your hand in mine and I'm supported
My brain cries out for you but I dance on and on,
alone
I move for you

It's late
I think the band in East Cove will be
playing their encore
We go to another bar.
I feel overwhelmed
I'm drained,
tired of the posers

I refuse to dance.
I think, the only way you'll get me out there is if Bruce comes on
I was sure he never would.

Not only does Bruce come on
but it's the spiritual version
I don't want to dance but I go out as a tribute to Bruce
and to you
I think, this will help me, I'll lose myself in the music
We begin
My heart pounds and my throat constricts

I hear the bells and the echoes
and think of you
I feel the drums and the bass go through my body
and think of you
I feel the struggle for life, our struggle, Bruce's struggle
and think of you.

It's lost,
all my feeling is lost
I dance on like a mindless creature who's numbed by
hate and sadness
The longer the song continues, the more my mind rages
The tears in my eyes are from fury

Another restless night

55.

I always have to rationalize to others what I was doing in the Cove

> I had the most beautiful relationship of my life, by rote, becomes
> Oh yeah, I had a great time

I'm going to write a book
It's going to be straight from
my heart,
my mind

I'm in a slump and it's getting harder to get out of it

I'm still schizophrenic
I bob merrily along or act real intense
it's not always an act, you know that
but I'm just real tired.

I wish you'd call.

56.

This time last week we were in bed
Held each other,
and I began what was
the longest day of my life.
Good, though.

57.

You're a hard habit to break

Sunday evening

58.

I imagine you sit opposite me
look at me
breathe life into me

I listen to music which is more than music
it carries our love through it,
like the rocks and water

I see a surrealistic sunrise which
hypnotizes
and yet,
somehow calms me

I can hear the water
and see the white, florescent spots in the darkness
They're ethereal, like us

59.

I've often thought of our first kiss
try to remember what I felt

I remember the feel of your arms
the curve of your body near mine
I could feel the nervousness in your mind,
not nerves perhaps but uncertainty
I remember snuggling in closer and closer
still needing to be protected from some unknown,
wanted you to do the protecting

I could feel us both relax
and then we lay back,
resting on the rocks
My body was turned towards yours
my head on your chest
To this day I don't know why you first kissed me
I only know that if you wanted to
I would kiss you again and again

60.

As I look back
I remember the incredible gentleness you're capable of and smile,
with tears in my eyes I waited for
Tom and Ken to go home
waited to see what would happen between ourselves.

You came to sit by me on the rock bench
I was nervous

You laughed softly
           I have visions of making love to you on the rocks, you told me
           Don't push your luck, says me

I'm not sure why
but when I woke up the next morning
I knew I would make love with you,
if you really wanted to

61.

I need to look at the stars with you

Chapter Four

September

62.

I walk home,
alone and in the dark
The sky is clear for the first time in days
Instinctively my eyes find the Big Dipper
I no longer need to search for it
I feel its position in the blackness
and use it to show me where home is

63.

I sit outside, on a small hill,
have escaped the noise and the lights of the dance
My eyes are bleary and it's hard to focus
but they find the constellation that's become
a landmark
for love
and pain

You find me laying on moss,
babbling about the stars
I throw your arm about me and cuddle close
It's the first time we're in loving, physical contact for more than a brief hug
I don't know how you felt but I knew only peace and happiness
It was the start of an extraordinary evening
full of many incredible scenes,
one as precious as the other

it was the first night I had to tell you I loved you, but couldn't
somehow I knew you would have enjoyed hearing those words
and I would have enjoyed saying them

When you came to me on the rocks
I held you as if you might leave me
By staying, you knew I loved you and I knew you
needed to comfort me
I knew my pain and confusion
was your pain your confusion
By simply staying with me
and touching me
I knew we would love each other for life,
even if those few hours spent together
at daybreak
on a cliff
were all we ever had.

Goodnight, I love you

September 5, Wednesday morning

64.

I come here,
hope to see you
hope for nothing more than
a knowing smile
a loving wink
but I sit alone
see you only in my memories,
which are all I have left

Wednesday night

65.

I sit in the bar
pretend you are here
You make me laugh and smile
God knows I could use a laugh

My heart wrenches
customers have come
our music isn't playing to just me anymore
I want to cry,
to feel as I do when I'm with you
to feel such pain,
such peace
I need to feel you against me
need you to hold me close,
to remind me that you haven't left
that you're still with me
fuck I hate it here
can you hear me scream

66.

What is it about music
I listen to Bruce and I'm immediately
in your kitchen
dancing
or doing dishes
getting primed for a big dance
cursing at people

I hold my kitten
Hope you'll come over to touch her
I love it when you talk to her while I hold her
It allows you to be so close to me,
without anyone noticing
I can feel you breathe
feel your hair
as it gently
breezes my face
or my shoulders
I can smell your skin
your hair
and when you rub her face with yours
I close my eyes
pretend it's my cheek you caress
my nipple you tickle

67.

I can feel the mattress beneath me
I can see the flowing curves of the bed frame
I can hear the wind blow
barely audible above my own breath
I feel the length of your body along the top of mine
We make love with our eyes open
Smile at each other the whole time,
except for a few brief climactic seconds

68.

I can hear the rain on the roof
but it no longer romances me
It beats upon tin
I watch and listen for a while
and as I listen more closely,
I hear it touch the leaves,
I long to feel the warm rain on my breasts

I want you in my bed and in me
I'm drunk and need your guidance
and your lips
I can feel your tongue in my mouth
and I can feel your mouth suck my lips
my head spins
I want you to materialize in my room
I want you here now
I need you to make love to me
I love you kiss me good night

I want to feel your mouth on my tongue
on my lips
I can feel your mouth
on my breasts
I wish the rain would stop
It would help me feel less lonely
I hope that you're alone

I need you to feel my loneliness
I need you to think about me
about my breasts
about my mind

I love you kiss me goodnight

I feel as I did on the nights I said goodnight
and then had to

walk up the stairs
alone
I love you

Make the rain stop

I love you I love you I love you
May God be ever at your side
I love you

69.

I get dressed to kill, mostly for myself
but also for you
I always think you'll walk into the bar
and my surprise will be great but relaxed

2:40 a.m.

The rain is beautiful and sad
I'm in bed under a warm feather quilt that hugs my body
The window's open ever so slightly
We listen to the sounds and breathe in life
understand one another's passion
know that this is our last night together

We touch, know each other's mind
       It's crazy, if we make love it would ruin everything, says me
       I'm glad you feel that way, says he

All we ask of one another is for a little peace and caring
We need to know that we are capable of touch and
love without guilt or fear

September 8, Saturday evening

70.

I'm tired of the struggle I go through everyday
tired of the front I must keep up
tired of supporting myself
No one knows
no one cares

I have spurts of energy
but they occur less often now
It's been over a week since
I've seen you
or spoken with you
It's beginning to exhaust me
Memories are, after all, just that
I don't really hear your laughter
I can only remember the feeling
it gave me
although good,
it sometimes rings hollow
I've forgotten the color of your eyes and that saddens me
I don't care whether they're blue or brown
I want to remember the subtleties and the changes
the sparkly shiny brown
or the warm caressing umber

I'm tired of not see you
I'm tired of telling myself to think of other things
My hands tire of reaching out to find dead air
My eyes strain to make you appear
My ears are useless because they can't hear you

71.

the wind lifts the branches like you lift my heart

72.

I know the feel of your arms
know the curves and the veins
I feel the love for your grandfather
I know your hands and how they feel in mine
I run my fingers along your forearms as they are
positioned on either side of my body
I speak to you about your arms
tell you I've always found them attractive
how long and lean they are
I'm pleased at your response
Goodnight, I love you.

73.

       Goodnight, I love you
I kiss you
and get a last tight hug before
I turn to go

You smile softly
I've frozen your smile in my mind
I stand in the doorway,
unable to leave you just yet
I'm happy enough simply to watch you
You turn over and sigh deeply

We laugh at ourselves
I see your body smile through the darkness
I walk up the stairs
feel crazy and happy
I crawl under my covers, alone
For an instant
hate and anger come to me
I hear you move
hear your father's moans and groans
and I fall asleep
unbelievably content with our decision

74.

I've been aware of you all night, he tells me during the dance

75.

Your voice reaches me
I hear sounds and textures,
barely able to concentrate on what you're saying

Your voice flows through my body
like your hands over my breasts

My fingers tingle
my eyes search for you in my kitchen
I this moment it's all I have of you
it becomes you
I feel your words more than I hear them

The moment you speak
memories as vivid as reality flash through me
I see things I'd forgotten
I feel things moments that faded
You are life
you revive me
I'm glad you called
I love you

76.

I'd like to be near you tonight
I need a hug desperately
I need to see you smile goodnight

You make me feel like a woman,
a fulfilled human
I've been told lately
that I look great, serene
Can you imagine, me serene?
I can

I wanted to tell you these things today
I miss having your attention all to myself
I miss the conversations
I miss you
I love you kiss me goodnight
The kitten's tongue isn't quite the same as yours
I'd like to tuck you in please
Goodnight, I love you
I walk slowly up the stairs

September 18, Tuesday 3:10 p.m.

77.

I've just spent a lot of time with you,
among many others unaware of our intimacy
Talk about the store brought back many strong memories
I'd like to be able to speak freely about them to you
but I can't
life won't let me

I wonder if you
remembered the morning we made love there
I feel sure you do but I need to know if you had visions of it as
I did, while you told everyone
about the upcoming weekend.
      You seem upset, you said at the time
      It's because I can't marry you and can't have your children, I replied

I laughed during that meeting
I felt the wonderful feeling that comes
from the knowledge that you've loved me and I'm content
I've known you in ways that others haven't
I'm delighted that we've been together,
that we've been lovers
I'm pleased most of all that knowing smiles and looks exist,
that I share secrets and experiences with you
that no one else does
selfish it may be
but I regret nothing
and secretly would revel once again from your touch,
should you desire me once more

78.

I cry softly as I think of the happiness you've created,
how many lives you've touched
sometimes I think mine is insignificant compared
to the others
but I'll learn it's not

There are things I want to say to you but I'm not allowed
I need a hug from you desperately
I need the support you so generously gave
And I need to feel the love you have for me

I've been alright lately but there are times,
like right now
when I'd give anything
to have the freedom to love you openly
the freedom to put my arms around you,
as I do with others who are my friends
but I can't
I'm not allowed
people will talk
people will get hurt

I tried to make up excuses to
keep you on the phone
but you took me so completely by surprise
that I could only half listen to what you said
I'm afraid of this weekend
afraid I'll snap at some point
I don't know what will happen

79.

I listen to our music
Allow only those to hear it who I feel appreciate it
but none really do
I listen to it with strangers
or I listen to it alone

80.

I hear the water all the time
I remember the last time we went to the club
the seas were wild with energy and life,
demanded us to take notice of
its power
its potential

The water is soft
it covers me as I lay on the shore
I feel each wave
first on my toes,
then move upwards
along my calves

A bit further,
and my knees are washed clean
I feel the coolness reach out for me
my breasts gently break the smoothness of the surface

The water reaches my neck and shoulders
I close my eyes
for an instant
my body is calmly submerged under
a clear coolness
that soothes
and exhilarates
My body is alive with thinking of you
The water begins its slow recession,
unravels the excitement it created
I lay uncovered, wait for you

I love you, kiss me goodnight

81.

My God, do I miss you
I sit here alone
alone with my little fluff of life
I look at her,
am reminded of strong violent emotions
yours and mine
I don't need reminders but
she is something real
she is not a memory
or an image

I wonder how much of this summer
I imagined
There are moments
when I can't believe
our other world existed
there was
as much pain
as love

It's crazy
but the love
wouldn't be so good
if the sadness
wasn't so deep
How can that be
I don't understand

82.

I leave the room no longer
able to contain my grief
I keep thinking,
rightly or wrongly
if she wasn't here
I'd be dancing with you
but I'm
no longer an intimate
no longer possess even the least freedom
my life is stifled and I feel
the unfairness
the hate
the love

I go outside, instinctively look up
    My God, it's dawn already. My God, it's the northern lights, I tell
    myself

I whimper
feel weak
I'm afraid
I manage to tell you the Lights are out,
forget that you've seen them before
    It's appropriate, ay? he says casually

I step into the night and simply burst into tears
no longer care about anything except
my loss of you and
how incredible life is
I sob on
and on
not sure where
or who I am
I feel my unimportance and
my weakness

I'm drawn by an unseen force,
as I was only once
before in my life
It controls me and I obey
I go to the rocks
Don't care if I die from exposure or
if I cause my own
death
I lay down and watch
My tears never stop
but this time, even I have to admit,
the pain felt good
I waited and waited
knew you'd never follow
Had you done so
you'd have expressed something
that I know isn't true
It really hit home
it really hurts
Sometime I would like to ask you
whether you knew
I was on the rocks
the rocks always help me communicate

We stand between the kitchens
        I shouldn't be here, I tell him
        It doesn't matter to me, he tells me
I stay because
I need to
I need to feel your arms around me
even though
they no longer caress,
now they console
I want you to hold me for the rest of my life
I think, my God, I can't remember the last time you
touched me like that
 Almost exactly a month

83.

She puts her paws
on my face
licks my nose as I write,
the way you taught her to
The thought brings
quick, silent soft tears

I know you've always
understood my need for her
and didn't laugh when
I called her "Cove"

I love you
kiss me goodnight

84.

I told you
I've lived with sexual frustration
before
but I've never awakened
so often in the night
only
to want
to feel another in my bed
to feel breath and life
to be reminded that I'm loved simply by
your presence.

85.

I remember wondering
if anyone would see the changes in me
not knowing how they would manifest themselves
last night a friend told me
really terrific things about myself
all I could think of was that I owe it to you
and The Cove
She told me I look great
am more confident
more important to me,
she said I seem really
serene
I can't think of a better word
to describe what
we've given me
Oh sure, life's a bitch lately
Including my withdrawal from you
but the happiness we created
is something that can't be
diminished by
anyone

Chapter Five

October

October 2
Tuesday after we saw each other in public

86.

It's so fucking artificial
we talk of superficial things

I want to ask you how you are
I want to be able to say
I feel like shit
Is it too much
to ask
to be able
to talk with you for more than five minutes

Oh sure, you call me for an hour and a half when
you're alone
and I can deal with that but
my God, the public superficiality drives me
crazy
I couldn't concentrate on you just now
I kept thinking
I need
to see you
alone

Sometimes
the worst part of it
is that I know
or I feel you know
that we both
need
these things

It's so frustrating
I hate it
we can't even talk about the

frustration
we're not
allowed
I love you, you know

87.

I hoped you'd call last night,
mostly because I thought you'd be in the Cove
no luck

88.

I feel so left out
Although lately
I create
my own
isolation

I've lost a lot of tolerance for people
I prefer
to be
alone

At this very moment our song has come on
the summer song of millions of others

I'm crying already
I miss the freedom
I had this summer
I miss the right to make personal decisions
I have no control
I have limitations put on me that
I hate

Why aren't you here
Why can't you be with me

I'll never be the same
I'm not sure
how it happened
but it did

October 9, Tuesday 10:05 p.m.

89.

The kitten and
I miss you
I need a hug

I made love with you in this room
I remember the feeling of freedom it gave me

Here you were,
not in The Cove
making love to me

I remember thinking
how pleased I was that
it must not only be
The Cove,
it must really be me,
otherwise you wouldn't
spend time with me in town
let alone
make love to me here in my space
I love you kiss me goodnight

90.

I awake
don't know whether
I'll see you before you go
Hope for a last brief chat

I open my mail
and realize
you've been thinking of me
          Give my love, you write, to everyone who matters

I feel included in that

Why is it that
we cry when
we're happy
it was partly
relief this morning
relief because I'm insecure sometimes
How can it be that a few words
can reassure me
give me back
my strength

It's crazy but
my happiness resulted
in a full morning's work
I was excited by my life once again

Sometime, I think,
I'll have to do it on my own
there won't be
words and notes
to support me
but for now,
I won't think about that

91.

Good night
it's nice to read,
          Give my love to my friends, in your note.
it's for this
I love you

92.

I lay in bed
the moon cuts across my naked body as it did one night
so very long ago
I miss you badly
Goodnight,
I love you

93.

Where are you
I need you
the bullshit goes on
my first impulse
is to call you
but I can't

94.

       I'm lost without him, says Frank

They love you,
as
I do

95.

I felt like Daisy Mae from the Dukes,
driving home with the boys
things are really quiet
I love it here,
chamber pots and all
you know,
I can't believe I'm here
it's not even for work but then
it never really was
I love you

96.

I love you
I'm still scared but
I'm here
without you
I had to come here when you weren't so that
I knew I could do it
I have
I love you

I'll be alright because everyone
I love here
also loves you

I feel more secure here than
I do in town
I love sharing a bed with the girls,
they're the little
sisters I never had
maybe I'm the sister
you never had
I love you
and I'm with you because
everyone in this house
loves you
Goodnight

October 18, Thursday 10 after 12:00 a.m.

97.

It was unbearable today
for some reason
I couldn't look at you
there was such a crowd
everyone babbling

I never even got a glance at you
I couldn't stand it
All I heard was
my own scream
my own wail
I hate it here
I want to be with you in The Cove
I couldn't move

I heard your voice
which means
everything to me

I hear you
and must listen
I see you
and must look
When you stand near me
I must touch you

I really needed you to
hold my hand today
I don't know how much longer
I can go on like this

98.

My friendships here are false
All day long people say things I disagree with
I don't know how much longer
I can ignore them

I need you to reassure me I'm
on the right track
I have no patience for selfish
people
people who are vicious
people who talk without speaking
I hate it here
Hate the insecurity
I've never been so alone

99.

I've become my own island in the stream
only you broke through the surface
only you have taken refuge there

I love you
hold me tight
I need to sleep close to you
need the security you bring

You're probably asleep in my bed right now
I love you kiss me goodnight

100.

How can people be so materialistic
I hate them
they complain about things they have no right to

I've already begun to show my intolerance
Why should I feel guilty about saying my piece
It's absurd
I know what's right and wrong
I know what it means to be self-less
these people are corrupt
I prefer to be alone with my thoughts

101.

I sit at the window
the fog weighs me down
It enhances my sense of suffocation
My kitten in my lap
watches me,
purrs and
plays quietly

The tears begin to well up
I don't cry loudly but
the loneliness
oppresses me
it weakens me

102.

My God, do I need to talk with you in a quiet place
where I don't have to pretend that I don't love you.